D0994987

MANAGING YOUR TIME

Managing Your Time

A Practical Guide to Managing
Your Time More Effectively

STEVE CHALKE
with
Penny Relph

KINGSWAY PUBLICATIONS
EASTBOURNE

ISBN 0 85476 469 0

*The material in this book has been gathered from a
variety of sources, predominantly informal
seminars and conversations, over the course of the
last twenty years. Tracing those sources would
prove impossible as, with the following exceptions,
no part of the book has consciously been influenced
by any particular book or article.*

*The quotation by Jonathan Steinberg on pages
65–66 is taken from* Effective Time Management
by John Adair (Pan 1988), p. 64.

The ABC grid on page 72 is adapted from
Managing Your Time *by Lothar J. Seiwert
(Kogan Page 1989), p. 57.*

*The Human Function Curve diagram on page
104 is adapted from* Managing Pressure At
Work *by Helen Froggatt and Paul Stamp (BBC
Publications 1991), p. 13.*

Designed and produced by Bookprint Creative Services
P.O. Box 827, BN21 3YJ, England for
KINGSWAY PUBLICATIONS
a division of Kingsway Communications Ltd
Lottbridge Drove, Eastbourne BN23 6NT.
Printed in Great Britain.

Contents

To Nikki, Charlotte and Aredi,
who have all worked so hard
to help me manage my time.

Introduction

I clearly remember the first day I began work as Youth Minister at Tonbridge Baptist Church. Fresh from college, I was ready to change the world. I was set up with an office with my name on the door, a telephone and even a secretary. At last I'd arrived!

But things didn't quite go according to plan. As the workload increased, so did the pile of papers on, beside and even under my desk. And as fast as I could sort them out or shove them into the filing cabinet, more would appear. The office began to resemble a paper recycling plant in full production. In short, I was disorganised. In the resulting confusion, I began to miss appointments and even double-book myself. The minutes and agendas of important meetings would go astray. Vital documents and briefing papers would mysteriously disappear.

Bogged down by mounds of paperwork, and with no idea *where* I was supposed to be and *when*, I began to wonder if my dreams would ever see the light of day. The best that could be said about my office was that the ceiling was extremely tidy.

But help was at hand. A church member who'd seen my desk, and with whom I'd obviously missed one too many appointments, invited me to a special Time Management Day organised by a friend of his. I went along, but only reluctantly. I was convinced my problem was simply that I was overworked. I didn't see how anything I'd hear in this or any other seminar could possibly make a difference to my busy and complicated world.

Almost twenty years on, it is no exaggeration to say that that one day completely transformed my life. In fact, as life-changing experiences go, it was topped only by the day I became a Christian and the day I got married. I've worked hard to build on the principles I was introduced to then about how to manage my time and organise my life. They are the basic tools that have guided me in my work ever since.

Personality or profession?

Over the years, starting with that one-day seminar, I've come to realise two vitally important things about myself and the way I handle my time.

First, I'm a *naturally* busy person. I'm kept busy not so much by the pressures of work and my diary as by who I am. I used to imagine that the reason I was so busy was because of my job. Being a pastor has unique pressures, and I figured that it was the relentlessness of these pressures that kept me so permanently occupied. How could I say 'no' to any of the demands being made upon me without turning my back on the kingdom of God? How could I not respond to people who were so obviously in need?

But since founding Oasis Trust in 1985, I've moved from being a local pastor to a charity boss. And in the process, I've learned something fundamental about myself: it's me, not the job. I'm no less busy now than I was when I was working for a local church; in fact, if anything, I'm far *more* busy now than I was then. If the pressures on me had been linked to my job, they would have stopped when I did. Instead, they've grown.

What's more, my work has introduced me to people from all walks of life: doctors, lawyers, journalists, politicians, bankers, advertisers, company directors, police officers, entertainers, plumbers, social workers, home-makers, television presenters, taxi drivers, etc., and it has been a real eye-opener to hear *them* making exactly the same claim that my church leader friends do about the 'unique pressures' they are under that 'no one else could possibly understand'.

It's true, of course, that each job has unique pressures. But, in the final analysis, blaming how busy you are on your job is nothing more than a vain attempt to pass the buck. And if you are somehow hoping that the day will come when your job changes and the pressures ease, you're in for a big disappointment. Face it: it's you, not the job.

Burnout

The second thing I've learned about myself and my handling of time follows on from the first. I need to be in control of the way I work if I'm not going to risk burning out. Rather than letting myself be driven aimlessly by other people's agendas and the circumstances of my life, I have to plant myself firmly in the driving seat with both hands on the wheel.

Naturally busy people always manage to fill, and usually overfill, their diaries, no matter how many pressures are taken off from outside. Because we *can* do more, we do. There is always something more demanding our energy and our attention. So it is important to understand from the outset that effective time management isn't about helping you do things faster and more efficiently so you can cram even more things into your diary. That is not a recipe for success. It is just a recipe for disaster and burnout.

The chances are, you're reading this book because you have too much to do and too little time to do it in. The good news is, the principles and ideas contained within these pages really *can* help you to organise your life so as to get more done in less time. The bad news is, unless you are disciplined in what you subsequently allow yourself to take on, even though you'll boost your output and productivity, you'll still end up having too much to do and too little time in which to do it.

A vital part of effective time management is

knowing what to turn down, and at what level to pace yourself. Not everyone works at the same speed. Each of us has a metabolism that runs at a slightly different pace. For example, some of us can eat whatever we like and not put on any weight, while others of us only have to look at a bar of chocolate or bowl of ice-cream to feel the pounds instantly piling on. In just the same way, some of us can survive with just four hours' sleep a night, while others of us need the full eight. Some of us can produce work at an amazing rate, while others will always be slower. Time management is about making the best use of the little time you have, working *within* your limitations to improve your efficiency. It is not about kidding yourself you're really Superman. As the saying goes, 'Work smarter, not harder.'

A false hope

Time management is now an enormous industry. For some it has become the philosophy that governs their life. Maximising their time means maximising profits, keeping a firm hand on the rudder and fulfilling their destiny.

As Christians we should beware of buying into any system that promotes controlling our diaries as the path to personal spiritual fulfilment. For one thing, it doesn't work. For another, we should never let ourselves become so confident in our own abilities that we then forget where our ultimate strength comes from. And, perhaps even more importantly, we must never forget that human beings are far more than just inefficient machines. Life is about considerably more than efficiency. That's why, in the words of the old cliché, nobody ever wished on their death-bed that they'd spent more time at the office.

Nevertheless, controlling our lives and diaries is important. (In fact, it's precisely *because* it gives us greater control over our future that time management can all too easily replace God as the cornerstone of our lives.) The biblical idea of stewardship applies just as much to time as it does to money and other resources. What's more, many of us have great ideas about what we can do for God's kingdom – ideas that will come to nothing if we don't learn to make better use of our time and talents. If I hadn't learned effective time management before starting Oasis, we wouldn't have achieved half the things we have, and countless opportunities to show God's love in action would have been lost.

Under arrest in Rome, Paul told the Christians at Philippi, 'Everything I *can* do, I do only in the strength of the one who empowers me' (Philippians 4:13). Time management skills empower us to make better use of our God-given talents. Rather than drifting along in the stream of life – or torrent, if you're as busy as I am – we are able to steer our own course and frequently avoid the rapids. The more we achieve, the more we realise we can achieve.

The time to start is *now*

Many books have already been written on the subject of time management. This one gathers together the advice I've learned and road-tested through twenty years of experience. My main aim in writing it has been to present a basic, practical approach to managing time more effectively in the light of a biblical understanding of how God wants us to live.

Ironically, it has taken five years to write this book. Not, you might think, the best advert. But that's where you'd be wrong. In fact, the reason this book has taken so long to write is not that I *don't* manage my time, but that I *do*. If I hadn't been totally committed to writing it, I would have given up long before now. But it has always had to take a back seat to other, more time-critical projects. So rather than allocating it a huge chunk of time up front, I've given it much smaller time slots over an extended period.

This wasn't an easy decision to make, but I can't afford to become someone who spends so long 'preaching' his message that he never has time to 'practise' it. In *Good As Gold*, Joseph Heller's satirical novel about US politics, the President spends the whole of his first year in the Oval Office carefully documenting his actions for his memoirs. But the truth is, the writing keeps him so busy that he never actually has time to *do* anything. As a result, at the end of the year, all he has managed to achieve is to write a book about what he *hasn't* managed to achieve.

This book is different. It is a practical guide to help you get the most out of your time. And although reading it won't change your life, putting the principles it contains into action will. I don't claim that putting these principles into action is easy – after twenty years I still find it a struggle. But they do work. You're reading the proof of that.

At the end of the day, even our clearest vision won't amount to anything more than a pipe-dream if we never master the art of organising and handling our time properly, because real vision is more than just a knowledge of where we want to go – it's also a detailed knowledge of how to get there.

Real vision occurs when the harsh pressures of reality are integrated into our worthwhile dreams. I have written this book because the church needs more than just dreamers. Now, as much as ever, it needs genuine, focused visionaries.

Taking Stock: Should I Be Making Better Use of My Time?

You're reading this book for one reason only: you're not completely happy with the way you use your time. You suspect you could be making better use of it than you are now.

The people who use their time least wisely are often those who appear to be working hardest and longest. It is very easy to be busy doing the wrong things, or even the right things in an inefficient way. So the first thing to do is to take stock of how you presently organise your time, identifying the main reasons why you waste it.

As an exercise in standing back to evaluate your own strengths and weaknesses, fill in the following self-assessment questionnaire. Knowing your strengths and weaknesses is a vital part of effective time management, so there is nothing to be gained by rating yourself either too high or too low. Honesty really is the best policy: anything else is a waste of time.

Read each statement below and tick the box which most accurately describes you:

	Always	Sometimes	Rarely
1 I keep a written daily schedule of my appointments and tasks.	☑	☐	☐
2 I find it easy to say 'no' when I need to.	☐	☑	☐
3 I can always summarise my priorities in life.	☐	☑	☐
4 I know where everything is on my desk.	☑	☐	☐
5 I consistently delegate tasks to others.	☐	☑	☐
6 I don't put off unpleasant and difficult tasks.	☑	☐	☐
7 Meetings for which I'm responsible finish on time.	☑	☐	☐
8 I have clear direction and goals in my daily work.	☑	☐	☐
9 I'm continuously planning ahead.	☑	☐	☐
10 I prioritise *important*, rather than *urgent*, tasks.	☐	☑	☐
11 I keep my telephone conversations to the point.	☑	☐	☐
12 I finish the projects I start.	☐	☑	☐
13 How I spend my time is consistent with my overall goals.	☐	☑	☐
14 I don't waste time looking for things.	☑	☑	☐
15 I keep my attention focused on the job in hand.	☐	☑	☐
16 I tend to tackle paperwork the first time I see it.	☐	☑	☐
17 I deal with priority tasks at the start of the day.	☐	☑	☐
18 I control my time rather than letting circumstances dictate.	☐	☑	☐
19 Other people don't have to chase me to get things done.	☑	☐	☐
20 At the end of each day, I feel I've used my time productively.	☐	☑	☐

Your response to these statements should give you a pretty good insight into how well you understand what you are doing, and how productively you are working. The more statements you could respond to with a tick in the 'always' box, the better use you make of your time.

If you ticked 'always' for all or most of the statements, you probably don't need to continue reading this book . . . unless, of course, you weren't being entirely honest in your answers! (Though you might want to check it out and then hand it on to someone else if you think it will help them.)

If you scored mostly in the 'sometimes' or 'rarely' columns, don't despair. The fact that you are reading this book means you recognise the problem, and the rest of the chapters are dedicated to helping you improve your score. So read on....

Scratching where it itches

From your answers, now pick out the three areas you think you need to work on the most. The chances are, these are all statements to which you answered 'rarely', but the best way to know which areas to choose is to think which statements made you wince the most, and pick them.

Resist the temptation to pick more than three. Even if you think you need to improve in most of the categories listed above, trying to work on more than three at a time is a recipe for disaster. One of the key principles of good time management is targeting *realistic* goals. If you try to change too much at once, you'll end up being so swamped that you won't be able to change anything. What's more, you'll probably lose all your enthusiasm for change altogether. Rather than taking a giant step forward, you'll end up taking a giant leap back. So keep your list focused on three areas.

Now, for each of your three categories, turn the questionnaire statement into a resolution: e.g. 'I intend to keep my attention focused on the job in hand', or 'I'm going to tackle paperwork the first time I see it'.

1 ....
2 ....
3 ....

As you work through this book, make it a priority to improve in these areas.

A time log

The next step is to take a few minutes at the end of each day to compile a time log.

To compile a log, simply write down everything you did during the working day – e.g. phone calls, meetings, dealing with mail, interruptions, etc. – along with an estimate of how long each thing took and whether or not you had planned to do each of these things. Make a note of what you think each of these things achieved, and mark them on a scale of *high*, *medium* or *low* in terms of how effective you think they were. (Have a look at my example on the following page.)

When you have done this for a few days, stop and ask yourself the following questions:

- Does my day have an overall structure?
- What proportion of my tasks was planned?
- Did some jobs take longer than I thought?
- Was I productive, or just busy?
- Did I give myself enough breaks?
- How much time did I waste?
- How would I rate my overall effectiveness?
- What could I do to gain greater control over my time?

When you first try compiling a daily log, it will probably take around ten minutes to do, but don't give up: it is time well spent. After a week or two, you will probably find that how you actually spend your time is quite different from how you thought you spent the time. Reviewing your log after a few weeks more, armed with the power of hindsight, will give you an even better indication of how well you have spent your time. Eventually, you will find yourself evaluating how you use your time on a constant basis, without the need for a written log.

Time	Activity	Duration	Planned	Achievement	Effectiveness
9.00	Coffee/chatted with colleagues	15 mins	No	Team-building	Medium
9.15	Priority phone calls	20 mins	Yes	Schools project	High
9.35	Meeting with John Benton	65 mins	Yes	LEA funding	High
10.40	Priority phone calls	10 mins	No	Schools project	Medium
10.50	Phone conversation with Steve	20 mins	No	Questionable	Low

Moving on

Do you really want to make things happen, or are you content just to keep things ticking over as they are? Changing the way you manage your time will take both time and effort. Psychologists reckon that in a work environment it takes approximately twenty-one days to change a habit. So if you really want to change, perseverance will be essential.

But so will be incentive. All of us need some sort of motivation to change. What usually makes us realise we need to make better use of our time is the feeling that there just aren't enough hours in the day. Either we're swamped at work or we never get time to do what *we* want to do . . . or both. There is no point in learning to organise your time more effectively if all it means in the long run is that you're just as swamped as ever, but with a slightly higher turnover than before. If you don't learn to create opportunities to do the things you want to do, they'll never happen. And knowing that you will have the chance to do what you want to do is a powerful incentive for getting your days and diary under control.

So as you strive to work economically and achieve more with your time, set yourself an aim. What would you like to have time for that you don't at the moment? Sport? Reading? Evening courses? The gym? Perhaps it's getting to see more of your friends and family. Whatever it is, keep it firmly fixed in your mind, and regard it as your personal reward for becoming more organised.

SECTION 1: PRIORITIES

The Gift of Time
Time Management in Context
Setting Your Priorities
Setting Your Goals and Objectives

I

The Gift of Time

'If only there were more hours in the day' could almost be the anthem for much of modern life. There seem to be so many things to do and so little time to do them.

My friend Rob Parsons, Executive Director of CARE for the Family and a practising lawyer, often asks the people who attend his stress-busting seminars how many labour-saving devices they have at home. Electric iron? Every hand goes up. Hoover? Washing machine? Every hand goes up. Dishwasher? Almost every hand goes up.

'Did your grandparents have these time- and labour-saving devices?' he then asks his audience. Five hundred people shake their heads.

'And do you have more time than they did?' Five hundred people shake their heads again.

The very technology that was designed to help us

find time to relax has quickened the pace of our lives and added to the pressures on us. Rather than giving us the extra leisure time its manufacturers promise, new technology seems, if anything, to make us even busier than ever. Labour-saving devices at home are joined by computers, fax machines, answering machines, mobile phones and e-mail in the office. And though they may make life easier, they certainly don't seem to be making us any less busy.

In fact, you could be forgiven for thinking that the amount of leisure time people have in any given culture is inversely proportional to the number of labour-saving devices it employs. Instead of giving us more time, modern technology has hugely multiplied the possibilities open to us, almost exponentially increasing the number of choices and decisions we are faced with. Our lives are becoming steadily busier and more complex. We seem to be locked into a battle against time – a battle many of us appear to be losing.

All this and more

Bill is an insurance broker in a large City firm. His already stressful job is made even harder by rumours that a corporate merger may be in the pipeline, inevitably meaning a whole sheaf of redundancies. Many of his colleagues are younger than he is, and most of them work late, often taking work home. Spurred on by a vague, half-remembered under-standing of the 'Protestant Work Ethic' and a genuine desire to work hard 'for the glory of God' – not to mention the need to support his wife and family – Bill ends up doing the same. In an effort to stay one step ahead of the game and his colleagues, he starts coming in earlier and leaving later.

This inevitably puts more strain on his family. He has been married to Sarah for ten years, and they have two lively boys aged six and four. Sarah recently discovered she was pregnant with their third child, scuppering plans to return to work as a nurse as soon as their youngest started school. She helps to run a local Mums & Toddlers group, as well as being involved in various things that need someone who is 'around during the day'. It may not be paid, but it is certainly work. By the time Bill gets home in the evening, both of them are usually exhausted.

In today's moral climate, Bill appreciates the need for him to make 'quality time' in his roles as husband and father, but the longer office hours means that some days he doesn't get to see his children at all. Sarah often ends up feeling like a lone parent. She and Bill argue far more than they used to, and never seem to have time to relax. Bill wonders how they are going to cope with the new arrival, but voicing his concerns to Sarah only makes things worse.

A large chunk of Bill's time is taken up with their local church. He not only leads a weekly home group, but also helps out as a member of the finance team and sometimes even preaches. He finds it increasingly difficult to meet all the requirements made of him, and spends most of his waking hours feeling guilty about what he's *not* doing. Week after week, the sermon highlights yet another area of life in which he appears – at least to himself – to be failing miserably:

- **Prayer.** After the vicar warns the congregation about the dangers of neglecting 'fervent prayer', and reminds them of the importance of the regular Friday night prayer meeting, Bill makes a special effort to get there. This involves him going straight to the church hall from work, grabbing a quick burger on the way. Another night when he won't get to see his children.

- **Family.** The following week, the sermon is on the importance of family life. Only too aware that he doesn't spend enough time with Sarah and the boys, Bill decides to leave work earlier and take less home. He knows that his sons are at the age when spending time with them is especially important, and he makes it a priority over work. His boss and his colleagues begin to notice.

- **Work.** Then Bill picks up a new book that stresses the importance of being a shining light in the workplace. Bill starts to wonder if he's not neglecting both his God-given responsibility to work to the best of his ability, and his role as a 'witness' to those at the office. When he overhears two of his colleagues remarking on how 'part-time' he is these days, he redoubles his efforts and stays later. If nothing else, he can't afford to lose his job.

Sarah and the children depend on him. But the long days and late nights really begin to take it out of him.

- **Health.** Bill starts to feel more and more tired and stressed. He knows his body is a 'Temple of the Holy Spirit'. He also knows he is not eating well, becoming more and more reliant on fast food and snacks to keep him going. And though he used to be a regular at his local gym, he hasn't made it down there in quite a while. He decides to get up half an hour earlier and go for a run in the mornings before leaving for work.

- **Quiet times.** Then, at the quarterly home group leaders' meeting, everyone is reminded of how vital it is to spend time with God each morning: praying, listening and reading the Bible. 'How can we set a good example for the people in our groups,' one person asks, 'if we're not spending quality time with God ourselves?' Bill resolves to make it a priority to spend twenty minutes in the mornings in prayer and Bible study. It means leaving later, but he can at least bring extra work home at the weekends.

- **Evangelism.** But the next Sunday the vicar draws him aside after the service to ask if he would join the Saturday Street Evangelism team. 'Support has been a bit thin on the ground recently,' he adds. 'I think someone in your position in the church could really help motivate others to get involved.' Not sure how to fit it all in, he nevertheless doesn't see how he can refuse.

- **Friends.** The following week is a guest service, where all church members are encouraged to bring along a friend who doesn't normally go to church. Bill becomes painfully aware that he hasn't invited anyone. How could he? He hardly ever sees his friends or neighbours any more . . . he never really has the time.

Like so many of us, Bill juggles his time as best he can between the various pressing demands and priorities made upon him, but he often finds himself frustrated by the fact that he doesn't seem to be doing any of them particularly well. At the end of his tether, unsure of how to balance the competing demands, he just feels like giving up.

Time may be a gift from God, but it can sometimes feel like he has short-changed us. Deep down, we know this can't be the way God intended us to live. But what is the way forward?

2

Time Management in Context

Time management is about the practical principles and guidelines that can help you get the most out of your time by using it as effectively as possible. By giving you more control over your time, and using it to best advantage, it can improve both the quality and quantity of the work you do.

Some people find the term 'time management' a bit intimidating, but the fact is that all of us manage our time. Some of us just do it badly! Good time management will enable you to:

- gain a better overall perspective of how you use your time and skills;
- bring your main priorities more clearly into focus;
- develop a strong sense of direction in your work;
- attain your goals more consistently and systematically;

- use the time available to you more creatively, achieving more with less;
- develop your ability to deal with, reduce or even avoid stress;
- create more opportunities to spend time with your family and friends.

The industry

These days, time management is big business. As life grows more and more complex, the need for effective time management increases. Simple commonsense principles have been talked up and have spawned an entire industry, producing a vast array of books, tapes, diaries, planners, seminars and conferences.

And though, to hear some people talk, you could be forgiven for thinking that they are all you need to turn even your wildest dreams into reality, the truth is that time management techniques aren't a miracle tool. There is far more involved in turning your goals and ambitions into reality than simply managing your time effectively. However, effective time management *can* help you make the most of the opportunities that come your way, and genuinely mean the difference between success and failure.

Some Christians are wary of using what seem to be 'secular' business management principles. 'Isn't the key to working more effectively just to rise earlier, spend longer in prayer and depend on God for the rest?' they ask. Well, not necessarily. After all, God himself is a strategist, so planning how we use our time and energy, and steward our resources, is simply imitating him.

In fact, far from being alternatives, dependence on God and careful time management are complementary. Our prayer should deepen our faith, and our faith is instrumental in helping us set our priorities, but there's more to good time management than just establishing priorities.

John Wesley was renowned for saying that he sometimes found himself so busy that he just had to spend an extra hour in prayer in the mornings. Without sufficient prayer, he reasoned, his days would lack the focus needed for him to get everything done that had to be done. There is a rich vein of truth in this, of course, but his failed marriage – he may have made time for prayer, but not for his wife – suggests that the policy wasn't entirely successful. In spite of his obvious prayerfulness, perhaps even Wesley could have benefited from thinking through his use of time more carefully!

Many Christians, however, aware of Wesley's achievements but not the toll they took on his home life, misguidedly quote him as irrefutable evidence that another twenty minutes of prayer squeezed into their day will somehow magically transform their lives. But all this really displays is an immature attitude to prayer, expecting God to sort out our problems for us rather than working with us to find a solution. Prayer doesn't remove the need for action –

quite the reverse: it reinforces it. The truth is, we are more likely to find extra time for prayer by improving our time management skills than we are to improve our time management skills by spending extra time in prayer.

In fact, some of the earliest advocates of time management methods were the English Puritan preachers. They were keen to give their church members practical advice about how to use their time wisely, suggesting that people keep journals to help them evaluate their effectiveness. Their descendants in the more secular society of the eighteenth century didn't abandon the principles; they just changed the ends. In place of enjoying and serving God, they substituted the goals of health, wealth and happiness. Rather than abandoning the discipline of time management, we need to redeem it. After all, at the end of the day, it is just a form of effective stewardship.

The good steward

'Time is money' is the motto of all stressed-out business executives who judge time according to its ability to produce money. But the analogy was originally used by Benjamin Franklin as long ago as 1745. Money was understood as a measurement of value, and both time and money were seen as valuable and limited resources. However, that is about as far as the similarity goes. Any further comparison devalues time, because it is infinitely more valuable than money. Put bluntly, the person with plenty of time but no money has everything to play for, but the person with plenty of money and no time is dead.

Of course, if we really believe that time is more important than money, this should have enormous repercussions on how we use and invest it. We're pretty careful about how we use our money. We bank it, budget it, invest it, save it and try to spend it wisely. But imagine you were to inherit £5,000 a day for the next ten years on condition that every day you had to decide how to use that day's £5,000 – if you chose not to do anything with it, you would just lose it. Most of us would think it pretty irresponsible to do nothing. What a waste of money!

We are all keen to steward our finances as best we can. So why are we so unconcerned with the economical and effective use of our greatest resource: time? Each of us has twenty-four possibility-filled hours every day. But while we all work hard at trying to use our money wisely, we often end up allowing our time to slip through our fingers as the result of ineffective planning and organisation.

A flexible friend

How do we manage our time without becoming obsessed and controlled by our diaries? Here are three important principles:

- **Discipline leads to freedom.** At the age of ten, like many boys, I learned to play the piano. But I hated the lessons, and did everything I could to avoid having to practise. As a result, I was terrible . . . and still am, as anyone who hears me playing today will quickly agree. At the time, I didn't see why I needed to be so disciplined, though I now realise that learning basic techniques is essential if you want to be free to play the kind of music you like. It's the same with time. Once you have mastered the basic techniques of effective time management, and how to use them, you'll find that you are a lot more free to do the things you want to do.

- **Time management is your servant, not your master.** Obsession with time, as with money, is a very unattractive quality. You don't tell your friends the exact amount of money you've budgeted for 'miscellaneous social expenses' when you're offering to buy them a drink. And it's the same with time. It is often helpful to 'diary in' time for friends or family, but never give them the impression that you have only slotted them in to fulfil a duty and maintain a properly balanced lifestyle!

- **Flexibility is the key.** It is important to allow for interruptions. Don't be fooled into thinking they won't happen, because they always do. Suppose someone calls on you unexpectedly during the day with an urgent need. How do you react? Do you panic at the thought of it throwing your entire schedule and you losing control of your carefully planned day? Can you instantly assess your priorities in the light of the bigger picture? Some of the most enjoyable events of life occur spontaneously or unexpectedly. There is so much we can't plan, so try to build in margins to cope with the unexpected.

3

Setting Your Priorities

What would you say if someone asked you to list the most important things in your life?

Being clear about what matters most to you is probably the biggest time-saver you could have. Knowing your priorities, and being able to focus your energy on achieving them, is essential if you are going to live life with purpose and direction, not just muddle through, being blown around by the winds of circumstance.

Imagine arriving for work one Friday with two major tasks – writing a vital outstanding letter and preparing for a crucial Saturday presentation – and a critical meeting ahead of you. As you start writing the letter, the post arrives. Opening it up, you find a final reminder for an invoice you thought you had already paid. It takes you almost half an hour to convince the company that you did indeed pay it, and just as you're starting the letter again, the phone rings. A colleague has a personal problem and needs your advice. You chat about it for a while before realising it would be much better to discuss things face to face. You agree to meet for lunch.

By now it's time to prepare for your meeting, which promises to be quite tricky as the person who is coming to see you is renowned for being unable to see anyone else's point of view. You agreed to the meeting as a favour for a friend, but it now seems more like an annoyance. To make matters worse, they are late and the meeting runs on for an hour. By the time it's finished, you feel like you have wasted an entire morning.

Your colleague arrives for lunch, so you head down to a local restaurant. Because of the personal nature of the conversation, you feel it's better to have lunch away from the office, even though you are starting to feel the seconds tick away. You try to concentrate on what your friend is telling you, but half of your brain is still trying to do a rough draft of the letter. You realise you may have to finish it on Monday.

After lunch, you start making notes for your talk until another colleague drops in to chat about a project you are both working on next month. An hour later, you are excited about the possibilities of the new project, but hit by the fact that it's late on a Friday afternoon – the least productive part of the week – and you haven't made a serious start on tomorrow's presentation. The next two hours are hard-going, and you're just beginning to get a handle on things when you notice that it's 5.45 pm and you're going to be late home for supper with your family.

As you walk out of the office, you're filled with a deep sense of frustration at everything you haven't managed to achieve. You know you are going to have to work long into the night to get the presentation finished, and you know that will annoy your spouse, who is looking forward to spending the evening curled up with you in front of the television.

Can you relate to this sort of day? If so, keep reading, because it's actually only a symptom of a much bigger problem. It is always hard to balance your own agenda with the various outside demands made on you, but unless you are clear about what matters most in the bigger picture, it will be virtually impossible for you to prioritise things on a daily basis. People who lack a clear vision of where they are going tend to spend a much larger proportion of their time simply reacting to the demands of others. As a result, they often drop the ball when it comes to achieving their key tasks.

Working out what matters most to you is an essential part of using your time effectively. Without clear priorities you will:

- always find it hard to distinguish between the urgent and the important;
- always struggle to keep your head above a rising tide of trivia;
- always be driven by other people's agendas;

- always feel frustrated by a lack of achievement;
- always be prone to anxiety and stress.

Before getting down to the practicalities of managing your time on a daily basis, it's vital to take a step back to get a wider perspective on your life. This is sometimes referred to as 'helicopter vision', simply because it gives you an 'aerial' perspective on where you're headed, and acts as a yardstick to help you distinguish between the important and the urgent.

First things first

'Do as I say, not as I do' is a well-known catch-phrase. We'll often *say* that something is important to us, but the way we actually spend our time gives the lie to this. Defining our key priorities is the first step in helping us to see whether the way we live matches what we say matters most to us.

Of course, there are a number of different sorts of priorities: those we set for a lifetime, a year, a month, a week or a day. It is vital to start with the big picture, because everything else will then be prioritised and assessed according to how it fits into our long-term plans. Until we have a clear grasp of our long-term goals, we'll never be in a position to understand whether what we're doing in the short term is meaningful or not.

For example, a high achiever like John Wesley certainly made time for the grandest of accomplishments – he had more than 400 different publications to his name, travelled in excess of 4,000 miles a year and, by the end of his life, had preached over 40,000 sermons. He changed the face of the Anglican Church and virtually reinvented evangelicalism, but only at the expense of a marriage. His brother Charles, who had warned him not to get married in the first place, knew that John would never make the compromises necessary to ensure a successful marriage, and was far from convinced that he had chosen a suitable bride. Charles' own marriage, by contrast, was a happy one, but his legendary devotion to his wife cost him equal billing in the history books. Charles is remembered for his hymns; John changed the world.

You can't have your cake and eat it, as they say – with time as with everything else in life. You have to make some fundamental decisions, because you can't do everything. Relationships and families take a massive investment of time if they're going to work, and have to be assigned a high priority in the bigger picture. If you want to be a good husband, wife, parent or friend, you'll have to settle for achieving less careerwise than you might have done otherwise. There just aren't enough hours in the day to reach our full potential in all directions.

The tragedy is that most of us *don't* think about it until it's too late. How many of us only really appreciate the importance of family and friends – and the amount of time we have to spend with them – with the benefit of hindsight? How many of us miss out on some of the most important moments in our children's lives because we've made them too low a priority in ours? Children grow up fast, and if we're not just as disciplined about making time for them at home as we are about organising our diaries at work, we'll not only shirk our responsibility as parents, we will also miss out on building the kind of relationship with our kids that will ensure they make time for us when they're older and the shoe is suddenly on the other foot.

The years you have with your children will be over and gone before you know it, so use them wisely and well. Though you may wonder now how on earth you're going to make the time in the midst of your hectic schedule to read them a bedtime story, play with them in the park, take them to a football match, or go with them to the cinema or McDonald's, the day will come – and sooner than you think – when you will desperately want to read them a story, but *they* will be too busy . . . not to mention too old. Rather than you trying to fit *them* into a busy diary, they will be the ones trying to make time to come and see *you*.

What lives on?

Alfred Nobel, the nineteenth-century explosives genius who invented nitroglycerine, detonators, dynamite and gelignite, never liked himself very much. But the wealthy Swedish industrialist liked himself even less one morning in 1888, when he found himself reading his own obituary in his daily newspaper. A careless journalist had unwittingly got him mixed up with his recently deceased brother, so Alfred Nobel had the rare privilege of seeing himself as the world saw him – a multimillionaire recluse who had amassed great wealth from the manufacturing of weapons.

Nobel, of course, had originally invented his explosives for peaceful use in mining and road-building, and he had long been troubled by their lucrative military application. Shocked that his whole life could be summed up so negatively, and with such ugly motives placed on him, he resolved to do something about it. Adamant that this wasn't how he wanted to be remembered when his obituary was written for real, Nobel set about changing his will to ensure that, when he died, the bulk of his vast fortune would go to fund the prizes that bear his name in physics, chemistry, medicine, literature and, most importantly of all, peace.

Most of us drift through life without ever really identifying what we want to achieve. What sort of mark do we want to leave behind when we die?

When fifty people over the age of ninety-five were asked, 'If you could live your life all over again, what would you do differently?' three answers consistently emerged:

- 'I'd reflect more.'
- 'I'd risk more.'

- 'I'd do more things that would live on after I'm dead.'

Well, you now have just such an opportunity to reflect. Like Alfred Nobel, you have the chance to think carefully about how you would like people to remember you after your death – only you don't have to wait until you're reading your own obituary in the newspaper to do so. Try to crystalise in your mind the things that matter most to you, and how you relate to them.

Now write down three things you would like to achieve with your life – three things you would like people to be able to say about you after you're dead and gone. They could be personal (e.g. 'I want to be a good friend to everyone who knows me'), parental (e.g. 'I want my children to know how special they are and how much I love them'), professional (e.g. 'I want to be an understanding boss'), practical (e.g. 'I want to be someone who can be relied on in a time of crisis'), pastoral (e.g. 'I never want to give people the impression they're imposing . . . even when they are!') or prophetic (e.g. 'Like King David, I want to serve the purposes of God in my generation').

1 PROPHETIC ....
2 PRACTICAL ....
3 ....

Having written down the things you most want out

of life, and what you'd like people to be able to say about you after your death, you can then work backwards from this list to determine how you can organise your life in order to achieve what you want.

4

Setting Your Goals and Objectives

To turn your priorities from a vague wish-list of the things you'd like to achieve into practical reality, you need to set yourself some attainable and carefully thought out goals and objectives.

Before setting out on a journey, every traveller needs to know three things:

- their starting point – where they are to begin;
- their destination – where they want to get to;
- their route – how they're going to get there.

Only when they're fully aware of both their destination and starting point can they hope to work out a sensible route.

If you have already read the earlier section 'Taking Stock: Should I Be Making Better Use of My Time?' then you'll have begun to evaluate where you are to begin. And the wish-list you supplied at the end of the last chapter, listing your priorities and how you'd like to be remembered, answers the question: Where do I want to get to? So now it is time to work out what route you're going to follow to get there: your goals and objectives.

Terminology can sometimes be confusing. At first glance, 'goals' and 'objectives' appear to mean the same thing. But (at least in the way they're used in this book) there is a big difference:

Priorities
The things that matter most to you in life,
and how you'd like to be remembered

Goals
Practical, attainable ways to ensure these
priorities are reflected in your everyday life

Objectives
Shorter, broken-down steps you need
to take in order to achieve your goals

Our goals give us purpose and direction in life. They are how we translate our priorities into practical steps for action. Without them, all we can do is drift through life, reacting to events as they happen but unable to link our response into any kind of overall strategy or plan. Regardless of how organised we may be, or how good we are at handling life on a daily basis, it is virtually impossible to be successful in the long term without clear-cut goals.

And to be effective, goals need to be specific. Few athletes would get up to train at 5 am every morning simply because they had a vague desire to become 'a faster runner'. But if their goal were more focused – winning a gold medal at the Olympics, for example – then they would have a clear vision to sustain and motivate them when the going begins to get tough.

Time out

Setting goals requires us to step back and consider our lives from a wider angle, rather than just being driven by daily pressures and circumstances. Only someone with clearly defined goals can retain a proper perspective in the hectic pace of everyday life. It is very easy to become so preoccupied with the present that you slowly develop a form of tunnel vision, unable to see the wood for the trees.

Making time to define and reflect on your goals is something that can easily get squeezed out of a busy diary. But it is important not to let it get overlooked. However much it seems like an unwelcome intrusion into an already overfull schedule, by showing you how everything you do fits, or doesn't fit, into the bigger picture, it will save you huge amounts of time in the long run. But the act of stepping back must be a deliberate one, and if you don't specifically book in the time to do this, you're unlikely ever to get round to it.

It is often useful to get away for a day or two in order to think through your goals. Sometimes being in different physical surroundings can help to create the distance from your everyday life you need to provide you with the opportunity to take a broader look.

For example, after thirty years growing up in the same small town (which you would have thought would have been long enough to prepare him for the difficult time ahead), Jesus still spent forty days in the wilderness after his baptism, praying and reflecting on the future, before 'going public'. What's more, his career was peppered with times of withdrawal from the public eye in order to prepare himself for what the future had in store.

Paul also spent time evaluating and re-evaluating his goals. After his conversion on the road to Damascus, for example, he spent several years taking a back seat before beginning his new role as an apostle. Having spent the first part of his life stacking up his credentials and carving out a career for himself as a Christian-hunter extraordinaire, he had to go back to the drawing board to work out not only what impact his encounter with Jesus would have on his faith, but also how to put his new-found priorities into practice.

Setting goals

No matter how grand it is, every goal needs to be attainable and defined in such a way that you can tell when you've reached it. It's OK to think big. Most of us are put off by the scale of some of our ambitions. But the truth is that whether a goal is massive or minuscule, it has to be planned for in just the same way: the bigger the goal, the more interim objectives you need, but the method is exactly the same.

The key is to devise carefully targeted goals, and then flesh these out into manageable, bite-size objectives (as I'll explain later). Each of your goals should still leave you wondering, 'How am I actually meant to do that?', but unlike your list of priorities, they should be clearly identifiable tasks.

So if one of the priorities you listed at the end of the last chapter was 'being a good parent', for example, you could break this down into attainable goals such as:

- spending more time with my children;
- constantly letting each of my kids know how much I love them;
- always telling my children when they've done something right, not just when they've done something wrong.

It's often hard to know if you're a good parent or not, but you can always measure how much time you're spending with your kids, or how often you tell them they've done well, to see if you're actually achieving your goal.

Choosing any of the priorities you identified at the end of the last chapter, list three goals that could help make it a reality, in order of their relative importance:

1 ....

2 ....

3 ....

Setting objectives

Once you have defined all your goals, it is essential to break them down further into short-term or easy-to-achieve objectives. As well as helping you to monitor your progress, these are the ways you actually go about fulfilling your goals, so it is important to give them a considerable amount of thought.

Above all, each objective needs to have clear parameters, and have incorporated within it the answer to three crucial questions:

• **What?** Be specific about your objectives, making sure that they are measurable and realistic. If they are set either too high or too low, they will fail to inspire you with much enthusiasm. They should be big enough to present you with a challenge, but humble enough still to be doable without exhausting you in the process.

- **How?** Unlike your goals, your objectives should be immensely practical and straightforward. Each one has to leave you in no doubt whatsoever as to exactly how it is going to be achieved and what resources you will need to attain the desired result.

- **When?** Each objective also needs a measurable timescale during which it should be done – a realistic deadline or frequency. 'As soon as possible' is too imprecise, making progress hard to evaluate.

For example, if one of your priorities was 'being a good parent', and one of the goals to achieve this was 'spending more time with my children', your objectives might include: 'always having breakfast with my children', 'taking each of my kids out for a meal alone once every couple of months', 'inviting one of my children to help me whenever I have to do an odd job around the house', or 'taking the whole family on a day trip to France some time before Christmas'.

Objectives need to be firmly set, but still flexible enough to cope with the unexpected. Just as a closed road would force you to make a detour, so circumstances will often require a change of approach in order to make it to your final destination. But it is always easier to alter an objective than it is to devise one in the first place. So start now. Taking one of the goals you listed above, work out three objectives that will help make it happen (again, in order of importance if possible):

1 ....

2 ....

3 ....

Playing to your strengths

One of the most important aspects of time management, especially when planning objectives, is knowing
your own strengths and weaknesses. Always check
that your goals and objectives make the most of your
strengths without depending too much on your weak
spots.

Carefully work out what you think your top three
strengths and weaknesses are. After you've written
them down, show them to a close friend and ask them
if it is a fair assessment, changing them if necessary.

Strengths: 1 ....

                 2 ....

                 3 ....

Weaknesses: 1 ....

                 2 ....

                 3 ....

The value of planning

Believe it or not, planning saves time. For one thing, if
your objectives are carefully planned, you know just

what you are meant to be doing next. Imagine the chaos that would have ensued if Jim Phelps, head of the highly trained and specialised IMF team in the 1970s television series *Mission Impossible*, had decided one week not to devise a plan beforehand, but instead just to make it up as he went along!

There are no hard-and-fast rules about just how long you should spend in the planning stages of a project before launching it in the open, but the basic rule of thumb is: the longer you spend planning a project, the less time it takes to execute it.

No plan works 100 per cent the first time, of course. You will inevitably have to re-evaluate your progress from time to time, checking to see if your goals are appropriate, your objectives realistic, and how often you hit your targets. Remember that objectives are just a means to an end, not the end itself. They are not set in stone, and will almost certainly need adjusting as you go along. Above all, it's important never to lose sight of your goals, even if this means taking a slower route to get there.

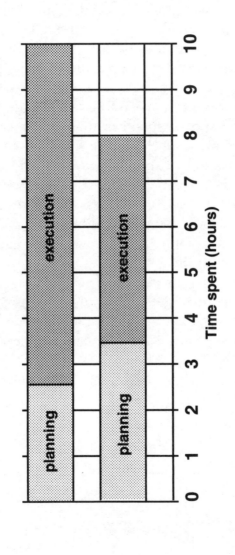

Time spent (hours)

SECTION 2: PRACTICALITIES

Planning Your Day
Setting Priorities
What's in a Diary
Clearing the Clutter
Avoiding Distraction

5

Planning Your Day

Knowing where you are going in the long term, of course, doesn't automatically guarantee success. As they say, 'A journey of a thousand miles begins with a single step.' You may know your destination, but you still have to plan your journey. You just can't expect to get effective long-term results without good-quality short-term planning.

Bringing order to your day, however, isn't as hard as it might sound. Though it may initially seem like an extra burden, the following exercise can reap huge dividends if you make a habit out of it. Once you are familiar with it, it shouldn't take you more than about ten minutes a day, and could save you as much as two hours! Remember: the more you plan, the more time you save in the doing.

Compile a list
  Learn to prioritise
    Estimate time
      Allow flexibility
        Review the day

Compile a list

Begin by listing everything you want or need to accomplish during the day, including fixed meetings or appointments, unfinished business from the previous day, any new work, telephone calls to make, letters to write, people to speak to, and any personal commitments or jobs you have lined up to do.

The best time to compile a 'To Do' list isn't actually first thing in the morning, but when you finish work on the previous day. It gives you the chance to evaluate your progress and prepare for the next day's work, letting your subconscious mind work on the problems overnight while you relax and enjoy what's left of your evening. Especially if you have children who aren't that interested in *your* homework but usually want help with *theirs*, compiling a 'To Do' list before you leave the office can be a very good way of signing off for the day at the same time as beginning to prepare yourself for tomorrow so that it doesn't take you by surprise.

The next morning, with your main tasks already in focus and possible solutions in the background, you can begin the day with a positive mental attitude. If you wait until you get to work to write your 'To Do' list, there is a danger that it will be too hurried and too late, as other activities start to crowd in and get in the way.

Learn to prioritise

You can't do everything, so you will have to make some hard decisions in order to determine the most important things you need to do. By using the ABC priority rating I describe in the next chapter, you will be able to recognise and deal properly with what matters most, rather than just reacting to everything the day throws at you. Learning to prioritise is a vital skill.

Estimate time

Estimate how long each of your tasks will take, and write down this length of time next to the task. Not only will this give your day its basic structure, it will also help you work in a more concentrated way. Deadlines are a very good way of focusing the mind on the task ahead, because most jobs will expand or contract to fit the available time. After all, there was never anything like impending disaster to spur on Scotty, the USS Enterprise's chief engineer in *Star Trek*, to fix the ship's engines fast.

- **Be realistic.** It is easy to underestimate the amount

of time and energy each task will require, so make sure you don't bite off more than you can chew. Start by recording the duration of your fixed commitments (e.g. meetings), then see how much 'uncommitted' time you have left to play with. This is the only really flexible time during the day, so use it wisely. Don't try to fill more hours than you've got. Book the priority things you want to achieve into specific slots, and fit whatever else you can in around them. What you can't do, don't do.

- **Group similar tasks together.** You can group tasks together either according to their nature or according to the overall goal they are part of. For example, if you have six telephone calls to make, you might as well do them all in the same chunk of time. On the other hand, if you have four things to do that all relate to the same goal or objective, doing them one after the other will mean that you maintain your train of thought and are probably more productive at each.

- **Build in a 'buffer zone'.** The nature of your work will determine how much of it you can actually plan or control, but you should always allow time for the inevitable unexpected tasks that crop up: phone calls you weren't expecting or visitors showing up out of the blue, for instance. You should always aim to construct a dayplan that will challenge you, but not prove so hard to keep up with that it eventually becomes depressing.

- **Give yourself time to relax.** There is more to life

than work, and part of the discipline of effective time management is giving you more time to do the things you want to do, not just increasing the amount of work you can accomplish. If you don't learn to relax and take it easy once in a while, you will simply burn out . . . and, if nothing else, that is very bad for productivity!

Allow flexibility

Always remember that a structured daily planner is your servant, not your master. If your life is anything like mine, something important often crops up that throws my daily schedule into total chaos. 'What matters most now?' is a question you need to ask yourself throughout the day. The answer will depend on the constantly changing circumstances and the needs of the minute.

Beware of becoming too rigid, without the flexibility to cope with the unexpected. If you're not careful, you will end up losing the very freedom you devised your day planner to help you achieve, as Dr Jonathan Steinberg points out. Rather than you controlling your time, your time will control you:

The unexpected caller, pleasant or unpleasant, disturbs the pattern of your time. That time is already allotted. Hence there is no time to help somebody who needs it, to relax and enjoy a chat on the street.

Enjoyment is always for *after*, when all the jobs with

deadlines, the letters to be answered, the calls to be made, have been despatched. But that time never comes. There are always more letters, deadlines, jobs and so life gets postponed until an indefinite *after* – until it is too late. A hamster on a treadmill has about the same sort of freedom.

Review the day

At the end of every day, you need to review your plan to see how you've done. You can do this immediately before compiling your 'To Do' list for the next day. The whole process should take no more than about five to ten minutes and will allow you to:

- keep track of the tasks you haven't managed to do;
- boost your confidence by seeing what you *have* achieved;
- increase your ability to plan your time by learning from your mistakes.

Have a look at the jobs that didn't get done, and plan when to do them. You should generally aim to complete any unfinished business the next day. If the same job keeps getting postponed day after day, either make it a priority or delegate it to someone who has the time to deal with it. If you can't do either of these, bin it!

We tend to be very aware of the jobs we haven't done and forget the ones we have. So look at what you have achieved, and encourage yourself by making a note of the progress you've made. If you only managed to achieve a small percentage of what you planned, you need to ask yourself the following questions to help you with your future planning:

- Did I underestimate how much time would be required for my tasks? If so, why? Did I miss something, or was I undisciplined in my work?
- Was I unrealistic in what I hoped to achieve? Was I just trying to fit too much in to my day, not taking account of my limitations?
- Were there more interruptions than I'd anticipated? If so, did I handle them well and re-plan efficiently?

6

Setting Priorities

'First things first.' It's a phrase we all use, but do we really believe it? Read the following pairs of statements, and tick whichever of the two you think describes you more accurately.

I usually begin each day with what's most important. ❏ *or* ❏	I usually begin each day with what I most enjoy doing.
I spend most of my time on my key areas of responsibility. ❏ *or* ❏	I seem to spend most of my time on urgent, but often minor, tasks.
The way I spend my day is mainly consistent with my long-term goals. ❏ *or* ❏	The way I spend my day depends a great deal on what crops up.

I generally plan 'uninterrupted' time in my day for tackling the major tasks. ❑ *or* ❑		There's rarely enough time for major tasks, which I then have to do at home.
Most days I feel I've done the majority of the important jobs. ❑ *or* ❑		Most days I'm frustrated about what I haven't managed to get done.

If you have mainly ticked boxes in the left-hand column, you're well aware of what matters most and you know how to prioritise your day to get the best out of the time available. But if the right-hand column describes you more accurately, it's time for a change in the way you organise your day. Don't worry: the prognosis is good. A whole new level of job satisfaction is just around the corner, and all you have to do is put in a little bit of effort to make it happen.

Most people muddle through day after day and month after month without ever realising that being busy isn't necessarily the same as being effective. Their days are crowded with urgent, time-consuming tasks that don't actually achieve very much. They gravitate towards all the more 'appealing' jobs that crop up, or those that broadcast their urgency loud and clear, rather than choosing the tasks with the most long-term productivity. As a result, they end up frustrated by everything they haven't managed to achieve, identifying with the writer who complained, 'Life consists of a series of accidents and setbacks that occur while you're trying desperately to organise something more significant.'

The key to maintaining a proper perspective in the hectic pace of everyday life is to establish your priorities clearly from the outset. Determining the relative importance of the various things you've got to do is *the* critical factor in deciding whether or not you'll be effective and efficient.

To do this, you will have to acquire the ability to discern between what's important and what's urgent. You'd be surprised how few things in life are both important *and* urgent. As you learn to prioritise your work on a daily basis, you'll learn to make instant decisions about the relative importance and urgency of things as they crop up. To be effective, you have to know what not to do as well as what you should be doing. Over-commitment is a guaranteed road to failure.

The ABC of priorities

Dwight Eisenhower, the World War Two general and former American president, is said to have been the originator of an ABC Grid (an adaptation of which is reproduced below) to help him decide quickly how much priority to assign to any given task, based on two criteria:

- Its *urgency* – how soon it had to be done, if it was going to be done at all.
- Its *importance* – how crucial it was to the overall strategic plan.

High Importance

B tasks
Timetable for action

A tasks
Act immediately

D tasks
Dump

C tasks
Timetable one or two; delegate or dump the rest

Low

Urgency

High

A tasks are both urgent and important, and should be given top priority. You'll need to tackle them personally and immediately.

B tasks are important, but not urgent. They don't need to be tackled immediately, but should be timetabled into your diary. B tasks should account for the majority of the jobs you do if you're using your time wisely. Only some will be suitable for delegation.

C tasks are urgent, but not necessarily important. Those that can should be delegated; most should be declined. Only a few should be timetabled into your diary around the A and B tasks.

D tasks are neither urgent nor important. Politely but firmly decline them.

Many people waste a great deal of valuable time by failing to prioritise their responsibilities correctly. It is very easy to be fooled into thinking that something is important just because it's urgent. A task is *important* if it plays a key role in your overall strategic plan, helping you to fulfil your goals and objectives. A task is *urgent* if it has a 'sell-by date' – a tight deadline or small window of opportunity past which there is no longer any point in doing it. Things may often advertise themselves as being category A (important *and* urgent) tasks that, at least for you, are neither . . . even if they seemed so at first glance and were viewed as being so by the person who sent them to you.

You will need to analyse each task carefully to

determine the answer to two questions:

1 What does this contribute to my overall game plan, and what would happen if I didn't do it?
2 How swiftly do I need to move on this?

Practice makes perfect, of course, and this way of prioritising will slowly become easier with experience. But like reading all the way through an exam paper before starting to answer any of the questions, it is a crucial discipline. Skipping it is a dangerously false economy.

Before allocating them a time in your diary, rank all your tasks every day on a 'To Do' list using this ABC method. Build in your A tasks first, then fit in those that fall into category B. Once you know roughly how many A and B tasks there are to do – creating a 'buffer zone' of extra time just in case meetings overrun or something unexpected turns up – you can work out which C tasks you can afford to take on, and which you should delegate or politely decline. (Delegating jobs isn't the same as referring them. You are still responsible for the jobs you delegate, so if you're not willing to oversee their ultimate execution, don't delegate them. Refer them to others if you must, but make absolutely sure you decline them.)

Prime time

Another important step in ordering your priorities is identifying your daily 'prime time' – that part of the day in which you do your best work. Develop the habit of scheduling in your most important and demanding A category tasks for this specific time slot.

Everyone's performance level fluctuates during the day. But this has far more to do with your body's chemistry than with how much sleep you got last night or how many cups of coffee you've had already this morning. There are 'morning people' and 'evening people', and it's your biochemistry not your bedtime that determines which one you are. Some people do their best work before lunch, but then find their concentration tailing off a bit in the afternoon. Others are a dead loss before noon, but find their concentration gradually improving throughout the day, coming into their prime when the rest of us are safely tucked up asleep in bed. It is said that Winston Churchill, for example, did his most productive work in the small hours of the morning.

Most people, however, are either 'moderate morning people' or 'moderate evening people', which means they can adapt themselves to someone else's timeframe, although they still reach their peak in the morning or the evening. It is possible to have medical tests done to determine which you are, though most people instinctively know if they are at their best in the morning or the evening. It doesn't actually make much difference which you are, so long as you're able to identify when your concentration is consistently at its peak.

In the nineteenth century, Italian economist Vilfredo Pareto discovered that 80 per cent of Italy's wealth was owned by just 20 per cent of its population. Known as Pareto's 80:20 Law, this 'rule' has since been found in a number of other areas of life, including time management. Research suggests that 80 per cent of your most productive and creative work is done in just 20 per cent of your time: one more reason to ensure that you schedule your A tasks into the 20 per cent of your time when you're at your best.

7

What's in a Diary

Is your system working? Read the following statements and tick whether they are true or false:

		TRUE	FALSE
1	I keep my diary with me most of the time.	❑	❑
2	If anyone asked about my plans for the next three months, I could tell them.	❑	❑
3	I keep a record of the birthdays of those closest to me.	❑	❑
4	I could provide the telephone number of my bank in under a minute.	❑	❑
5	I never make notes of telephone calls on the nearest bit of scrap paper.	❑	❑
6	I haven't double-booked myself in the last six months.	❑	❑
7	I'm clear about my tasks for the day		

by 9.30 each morning.   ❏   ❏
8 If I have a good idea, I always write it
   down where I can find it.   ❏   ❏
9 I can tell from a glance in my diary
   what I'm doing this week and when.   ❏   ❏
10 I carry forward any outstanding tasks
    at the end of each day.   ❏   ❏

If your current diary system is working for you, all of
the above statements are likely to be true.

Spoiled for choice

A good diary – whether paper or electronic – is an
essential tool for anyone who is serious about
managing their time well. But just *having* one isn't
enough. It's a myth that anyone owning a Filofax or
Psion organiser must automatically be well organised.
There's a lot more to using a diary efficiently than just
opening it up or turning it on.

There are all sorts of diary systems and methods on
the market, some with their own unique language of
key symbols, accessories and courses. Some manufacturers promote their system as *the* complete way to
organise your life, with up to a 40 per cent saving of
your time. But in fact, like any tool, a time management system is only as good as the person using it. In
the hands of an organised user, it can save a
considerable amount of time, but in the hands of
someone less willing to be disciplined in their

approach, even the most carefully thought-out, hi-tech system is about as much use as a mail bag to a milkman.

Without knocking any of the commercially available systems, some of which I've used to great effect, you can be an excellent time manager without even spending a penny. So don't be fooled into thinking that your life will suddenly improve in leaps and bounds once you've acquired the latest, top-of-the-range, computer-enhanced personal organiser, because a system is only as good as its weakest link . . . and that could be you!

A look inside

The best type of diary by far is either a looseleaf Filofax-type or one of its electronic equivalents, and the most important page is the one you should place just inside the front cover – your daily 'To Do' list.

When you compile this, begin by listing all your appointments for that day (as explained in Chapter 5) on the left-hand side of the paper. Then list all the other tasks you have to do on the right-hand side, except for the big, important ones, which you should fit into the best slots around your fixed appointments. Tackle the other, smaller jobs from your 'To Do' list whenever you get a spare five minutes throughout the day. Most people waste all the odd bits of time because, when they've finally worked out what to do with them, they're gone anyway!

Today		To Do
		PHONE
0800		Fred Bartholomew
0900	correspondence	
1000	Meeting with Stuart Aimes	**WRITE**
1100	"	
1200	phone calls and letters	Letter to MRCI & Co.
1300	Lunch with James @ Le Diner, Brook St	
1400	"	**OTHER TASKS**
1500		
1600	Miles Nairn	Talk to Peter about the GT speech
1700		
1800		
	supper @ Jill &	
	Danny's	

Whatever kind of diary you use, make sure it caters for one-week-at-a-view, and also has hourly slots for each day. If you opt for a diary without specific time slots, you'll end up trying to cram too much into a tiny space, scribbling appointments down in the wrong order: dinner with Jill at 8 pm, arranged two months ago, will be written large in the centre, but a vital assembly talk at 9 am at the local school, booked only last week, will find itself squeezed down into the bottom corner. As a result, you won't be able to see how much time you have available in the day, let alone when. It will take you ages to decipher the jumble of scribble when you complete your 'To Do' sheet, and even then you might miss something. On top of all that, because your page is so disorganised, you will always run the risk of double-booking yourself.

Your diary should also contain a year planner. It is vital for you to be able to see at a glance what you're doing over a longer time period, just in case someone asks you to commit to something early.

It should also contain special pages for everyone you work closely with – e.g. a designated 'Mike' or 'Heather' page. Simply use it to write down everything you want to raise with them so that, when you meet them, all the issues you need to talk about are at your fingertips, rather than forgotten until it's too late.

Another big advantage of loose-leaf Filofax-type systems is that they allow blank pages for notes to be interleaved with diary pages, and it's both quick and

	Mon 21	Tues 22	Wed 23	Thur 24	Fri 25	Sat 26
am	John's birthday			Jill's interview		
8			Clare @ Snack			
9	correspondence	Larry & John /A	correspondence	Board Meeting/A	correspondence	Off
10	Stuart Aimes/B	–	call Anne Gil/B	–		
11	call Fred B./A	–	call Steve & Jo/B	–	Rachel B./B	
12	letters	correspondence	Terry Lloyd/C	call J. Fellon/B	Carrie & Bob/B	
13	James @ Le D./B	Paul/B	Leave for Derby	call Pete, Ann/B	–	Sun 27
14	–	–	–	letters	Peter McQ./C	
15		Do GT speech /A	–	–	Jeff Hanssen/A	All Saints
16	Miles Nairn/C	–	–	Robert Town/B	–	
17	–	–	–	–		Off
18				call Jill		
pm	supper @ Jill &		GT presentation	supper @ Jeff &		
	Danny's		(Black Tie)/A	Maura's		

simple to write things down and find them again. The disadvantage is that they inevitably become 'bulked out' if you don't prune the contents regularly, and this is where electronic organisers have the edge. Provided you've bought one with enough hard-drive memory, it can store the same amount of information in half the amount of space.

Your life in print

Writing things in your diary provides a whole host of advantages. It will help you:

- **Reduce your workload.** If you write down what you've got to do, you effectively reduce the workload for your memory. Your brain is freed up to think creatively about more important things, instead of acting as a diary. Don't make the mistake of trying to make 'mental notes'. If something is important, you can't afford to risk forgetting it; if it isn't, you're just cluttering your mind with trivia.
- **Reduce your stress levels.** Gaining good control of your time also means you will feel far less fatigued and stressed. You won't have to worry about missing appointments, and having all the key points of your life in one place will help your self-confidence. (Unless, of course, you lose your diary or the electronics crash! That's why it is always wise to keep a copy of all important information somewhere else. The joy of electronic organisers is

that you can back up information onto your main computer at home or work, or even onto disk.)

- **Focus your mind.** If you can see your tasks in front of you on a piece of paper or a screen, you will be less easily distracted and far more likely to persist in carrying them out.
- **Control your schedule.** Writing your daily plan will help you keep better track of all the projects and tasks you are responsible for. It will give you an overview, allowing you to plan and co-ordinate important projects in a systematic way.

Spring cleaning

Whether you're using a loose-leaf system, an electronic organiser or a conventional week-at-a-view diary (with a spiral notebook for your 'To Do' list), one thing you'll have to get into the habit of doing is reviewing and pruning it every once in a while. Exactly how often you do this – once a week, once a month, once every three months, etc. – is entirely up to you.

This allows you a golden opportunity to review your progress, evaluating how you are doing with the various projects you have on. It's also an excellent way of making sure that any notes, names and addresses end up where they're supposed to be inside your diary, and that you have taken a copy of them to store somewhere else.

8

Clearing the Clutter

It's 9 am Monday morning. You sit at your desk, ready to open the mail. As you gaze at the mountain of letters, brochures, magazines, faxes, printed e-mails, phone messages, post-it notes and dirty coffee cups, you remind yourself that you really *should* tidy it all up. You decide to do it later . . . once you've opened the post.

Today's mail contains two newsletters, several bits of junk mail, a letter from an ex-colleague and a reference form for a member of your church youth group. You put most of the junk mail in the bin, saving an interesting-looking glossy brochure to read later, filing it for safe-keeping in your already overflowing in-tray.

Looking at the newsletters, you realise you don't have time to read them, so you put them on the side of your desk. You start filling in the reference form, but realise after five minutes that it's going to take longer than you'd initially thought. Glancing at your diary, you see a space at 4.30 pm and pencil it in for then. Remembering you have an important call to make before 9.30 am, you put the rest of the post to one side for a moment.

Looking for a piece of paper during the call, you notice that you haven't replied to a wedding invitation you received last week. You look in your diary to confirm that you can make the date and see that you're supposed to be speaking at the end of next week to a church meeting on the other side of town. You recall that they need to know the title of your talk by Wednesday. You search for their letter of invitation, hoping to find their phone number, but it seems to have vanished into thin air. As you hunt through your in-tray, you find a Barclaycard bill that should have been paid three weeks ago!

Does this sound familiar? Do you sometimes have to clear a space on your desk just so you have room to work? Do you sometimes 'unearth' important pieces of paper at the bottom of your in-tray, only to realise that you've missed the deadline? Do you stuff your briefcase with papers, hoping to get a chance to deal with some of your backlog at home? Do you often handle papers several times before finally deciding what to do with them? And are you one of those people who occasionally has a huge clear-out, spending a whole morning clearing your desk of paperwork by dumping a lot of it in the bin?

If your desk always looks like something from an Ikea furniture catalogue – tidy and well laid-out – move on to the next chapter, but if, to be honest, it looks more like a bomb-site than a work station, read on. Handling paperwork efficiently and keeping our desk relatively tidy are two skills most of us struggle with. Despite all the predictions of a paperless society, we still seem to be drowning in it.

Seven steps to a tidy desk

The first step on the way to a tidy desk is facing up to the fact that things need to change. The next six are listed below:

■ **Plan and prioritise your paperwork.** Most people react to post or other papers landing on their desk the same way they do to the telephone ringing: everything stops immediately and their time is completely hijacked. So open your post and sort out your paperwork when you've planned to, not when it arrives. Ask yourself three questions with each piece of paper:

- Does it even deserve my attention? (If not, put it straight in the bin.)
- Is it better handled by someone else? (If so, give it to them.)
- Does it require action? (If so, give it an ABC priority rating and diary it in.)

■ **Deal with paper only once.** Ideally, each piece of paper arriving on your desk should be handled a maximum of twice. Research shows that a piece of paper left on your desk will distract you up to five times a day. So when a letter arrives, read it completely and decide what action to take. If you need to do something about it, put it in your in-tray and don't pick it up again until you're ready to deal with it. Take positive action with paperwork; don't procrastinate.

- 'Spot the difference.' If you need a little extra convincing, try this: for the next week, every time you pick up a piece of paper to consider dealing with it, spot it with a coloured marker. If your desk resembles an outbreak of measles by the end of the week, you need to be more decisive.

■ **Bin junk mail.** Believe it or not, your bin is one of the most useful pieces of equipment you have, and most of the papers on your desk will eventually end up there. The key to effective paper handling is knowing what matters and what doesn't. So don't use your filing cabinet as a half-way house to the bin. Be more ruthless! Don't even open junk mail, for instance – put it straight in the bin, still in its envelope.

■ **Work on one project at a time.** Whenever possible, work on just one project at a time, and remove all the paperwork relating to it from your desk before moving on to the next job. Provided all the various bits of paper on your desk relate to the same project, you're probably working quite effectively. But if they relate to lots of different projects, they'll not only distract you from the task in hand, they'll also get muddled up and probably be misfiled. Remember that 'clearing away' means filing in the appropriate place, not just making another pile.

■ **Don't accept unnecessary paperwork from colleagues.** Don't allow your colleagues to dump paper on your desk if they should be dealing with it themselves, and minimise the number of memos circulating whenever you can by hand-writing your reply on the same piece of paper and returning it. The same principle can apply to e-mail, where it is often appropriate to return the message with an answer, and delete the original message.

■ **File papers when you're done with them.** File all the material you've finished with for the moment but think you might need again some time in the near future. (Some papers need to be kept permanently for legal or official reasons, and these should be stored rather than filed, separate from your filing system.) A good filing system makes its contents easily accessible to anyone who needs them, because filing is about speedy retrieval, not storage. And remember: there is no such thing as an easy-to-run filing system. They all take time both to set up and maintain. But in the long term a good system will save you far more time than it costs. Remember:

- Label all your files clearly and systematically.
- Keep your file categories specific rather than general.
- Keep your files thin – no more than an inch thick at the very most.
- Never keep a 'miscellaneous' file.
- Clear your files at least once a year.
- Impose some logical order on your files, e.g. alphabetical, chronological, etc.
- Store or bin your old files.
- Start today!

9

Avoiding Distraction

No one likes being interrupted when they are working, but the truth is that the person who interrupts you the most is probably none other than you! It's possible to waste time in all sorts of ways: making non-urgent or unimportant phone calls; making yet another cup of coffee; dipping into projects, then moving on to something else when it gets too tough; hanging around chatting too much; not being disciplined in meetings; half-reading letters, then putting them on one side to deal with later . . . The list of time-wasters is a very long one.

Time-wasting is a skill that comes naturally to most of us. Here's how to master the top ten:

Top ten time-wasters

- **The telephone.** An all-time favourite. When you're struggling with a difficult chore, or about to get down to an important task, why not make a phone call instead? In fact, the phone can often be a 'double whammy' time-waster because the person on the other end may be just as anxious as you are to waste time. Try to spend as much time as you can on the phone, always answering it as soon as it rings and never using an answering machine to take incoming calls for you. Make your calls whenever you think of them rather than at a planned time and, above all, make absolutely sure they drag on longer than necessary.

- **Poor communication.** Another winner – hackneyed but still effective. To guarantee errors, misunderstandings, inefficiency and far more work than you started with, you'll need to ensure that you always give vague answers and never let anyone pin you down to a firm response when planning a task. Always skip a few vital bits of information, and try to avoid thinking things through logically. Don't leave things like this to chance. Make sure you never finish a conversation fully aware of what the other person was talking about and, above all, never get all the information you need for a task before you start it.

- **Losing things.** How much time do you spend each week looking for things? It's not just mislaid paperwork that wastes time: you can lose staplers, rulers, envelopes, memo pads, telephone numbers, keys . . . all sorts of things. You might not think there's much time to waste here, but you'd be surprised: just fifteen minutes a day searching for things amounts to an hour and a quarter wasted each working week! The trick is to be imaginative. Remember the saying, 'A place for everything and everything out of place.'

■ **Lack of discipline.** Whatever you do, never stick to the schedule you spent all that time devising. If you do, not only will you save time by working efficiently, you'll also miss out on the marvellous opportunity of making all that planning time redundant. Always take the short cut, remember you're a free spirit and never try to analyse how you use your time.

■ **Reverse delegation.** Spend just a few minutes a day cultivating the image of yourself as a troubleshooter, able to deal quickly with the tricky problems others shy away from. If a colleague comes to you saying, 'I've got a real problem here,' respond by telling them, 'OK, leave it with me and I'll get back to you.' Resist the temptation to become just an advisor and overseer on the tasks you delegate. Instead, ensure you wrestle them back from the person you gave them to, and spend as much time as you can solving them yourself. Remember the golden rule: don't delegate something if you can waste more time doing it yourself. Never let go!

■ **Interruptions.** Repeated interruptions not only stop us from doing what we're meant to be doing, but have a wonderfully disturbing cumulative effect. Once your concentration has been broken, it can take between five and ten minutes to regain it fully . . . by which time, if you're lucky, something else will have happened to interrupt you. Never book in uninterrupted time, especially when you are at your peak; and, harping back to time-waster no.1, never use the 'Do Not Disturb' button, answering machine facility or 'Off' switch on your phone. If you can't find anyone else to interrupt you, try interrupting yourself by following every tangential train of thought that comes up immediately, rather than writing it down on a memo pad and coming back to it later.

■ **Meetings.** Try to increase the proportion of your time you spend in pointless meetings, especially if they are poorly managed or, better still, completely unnecessary in the first place. Insist on going to meetings rather than having them come to you, and play deaf if someone mentions telephone conference calls as an alternative to face-to-face contact. If you're organising a meeting, don't write an agenda. If you're forced into doing one, make sure it is as confusing as possible and don't give anyone a copy until they are actually sitting in the meeting room. Try to avoid putting a finish time on a meeting; if you have to have one, ignore it.

■ **Procrastination** is another creative time-waster. All you need is some real or imagined spare time tomorrow, next week or at any point in the future, as well as something nicer and easier to do right now. Not only will procrastination make you terribly inefficient, of course, it will also add considerably to your overall sense of worry, guilt, pressure and low self-esteem, so reducing your efficiency even more. Obviously, the most effective things to put off are the 'nasty' jobs you like doing least and the big, important, time-critical assignments. One further tip: never succumb to the urge to break big tasks down into less daunting, more manageable chunks, and never let anyone give you a hand.

■ **Crises.** Work hard at cultivating the useful skill of turning a minor hassle into a major catastrophe, injecting as much drama and ham acting into the proceedings as possible. Never allow anyone to put things into perspective for you, but spend as much time as you can rushing headlong from one crisis to another. The adrenaline rush will give you all the job satisfaction you need, and it will disguise your time-wasting under frantic activity. And, by upping your stress levels, it will make you far less efficient and eventually force you to waste more time by taking sick leave because you can't cope.

■ **Perfectionism.** You'd be amazed how much time you can lose simply by adopting a real perfectionist attitude to your work. Never look at how this job fits into the big picture. Putting things into context can be dangerous. Instead, insist on getting everything 100 per cent right, even when 95 per cent will do fine. It doesn't matter that no one but you will notice the difference: it's a point of honour. Be finicky. Never let your standards drop below excellence, especially when excessive attention to detail will jeopardise the entire project. Stand your ground.

Redeem the time

Now is the time to start reversing the process of getting distracted by your time-wasting habits. The following steps should set you off on the right path. You can follow the same steps for any of them, although I've given the telephone as an example throughout.

You will probably find it hard-going at first, and you might have a relapse from time to time, so keep in mind all the reasons you gave yourself for wanting to manage your time better, and use these as incentives when the going gets tough.

■ **Name your top three time-wasters.** The first step is to own up to your problem areas and decide to take action on at least one of them *now*.

1 ....
2 ....
3 ....

■ **Assess the damage.** How much time do you waste? What other problems result from your habit? Taking the telephone as an example, try the following:

- Time your calls for one day using a stopwatch, noting what they were about.
- Ask yourself how many of them were productive. How many were unwanted or unexpected? Could some have been dealt with by someone else? Did you waste time rambling on about things of little importance?
- Estimate the amount of time your calls waste in terms of lost concentration, or being late for appointments/meetings, etc.

■ **Determine how you would like to be.** What difference would it make if you changed your habit? How would it make you feel? How much time would you save? Write down all the positive repercussions.

■ **Decide on a practical course of action.** What steps would you need to take in order to change? Still using the telephone as an example, they might include:

- asking an assistant, if you have one, to deal with all your non-urgent calls at certain times during the day, leaving you free to work uninterrupted. Otherwise try switching on your answering machine (if you don't have one, get one), or even turning off the phone. If a call is important, the caller will ring back;

- planning blocks of time in your day specifically to deal with telephone calls;
- setting time limits for the calls you make, and learning to stick to them;
- finding, and practising, polite-but-firm ways to keep incoming calls focused and to the point.

SECTION 3: PRESSURES

Working with Pressure
Controlling Stress
Beating Burnout

10

Working with Pressure

One of the consequences of the technological revolution that has taken place in the last half century has been an increase in the amount of pressure most of us are under. Fifty years ago, the pace of life and work was limited by the available technology. Few people could boast of owning a car, no motorways existed, trains were slower and air travel was limited. Not many households had a telephone, and most communication was by letter, which took time to write, time to send and allowed the receiver time to think things over before needing to respond. The limitations of the technology – however 'cutting-edge' it seemed at the time – regulated the pace of life, which happened far more slowly than it does today.

Life is very different now. Not just cars and telephones, but fax machines, mobile phones, e-mail and laptop computers are more or less taken for granted. Flying isn't just faster than other forms of travel, it can often be cheaper too! The factor that slows things down now isn't technology, it's people!

The irony is that the very tools which were designed to make life easier for us have actually added to its pace, and therefore upped the amount of stress and pressure we all live under. A recent MORI poll of the UK's top 500 companies showed that 65 per cent of employers believe stress is the main cause of ill health in the workplace. The number of workers taking time off work for a stress-related illness has increased by 500 per cent since the 1950s, and doctors estimate that anywhere between 50 per cent and 75 per cent of all health problems are either caused, or significantly aggravated, by stress.

Friend or foe?

Stress is caused by excess pressure, but pressure and stress are not the same thing. We all need pressure: it's an essential ingredient in helping us to work well. It makes us alert, clarifies our thinking and makes us more dynamic. Without the pressure of deadlines, other people's demands and our own high standards, we wouldn't achieve nearly as much as we do. Pressure sends adrenaline pumping round your body, helping you make good decisions, communicate effectively, act confidently and get the most out of life.

But the problem is that *too much* pressure has exactly the opposite effect. It becomes detrimental to your vitality, your relationships, your ability to listen to others, your openness with friends or colleagues, your physical stamina, your perception, your memory, and your overall emotional stability. If unchecked, it can create a host of physical and medical problems, including indigestion, headaches, muscle pains, tiredness, night sweats, ulcers and even heart disease, as well as aggravating existing conditions and allergies. It will even increase your susceptibility to accidents and your tendency to make mistakes!

Because pressure can have such a positive or negative effect on us, it is vital that we learn to use it wisely. Being aware of how it affects us is the first step to managing it well and ensuring that it serves us rather than controls us.

The ups and downs of pressure

The graph shown on page 104, known as the Human Function Curve, helps to explain the positive and negative effects of pressure. Too little pressure is never helpful. Under-stimulated people rarely perform efficiently. Rather than 'attacking' a day, they end up meandering through it. People who are unemployed or who work alone – church leaders, for example – can be especially prone to this problem. Pressure improves performance, and the *right amount* will optimise your effectiveness. Hence the saying, 'If you want something done, ask a busy person.'

But there comes a point – known as your 'stress

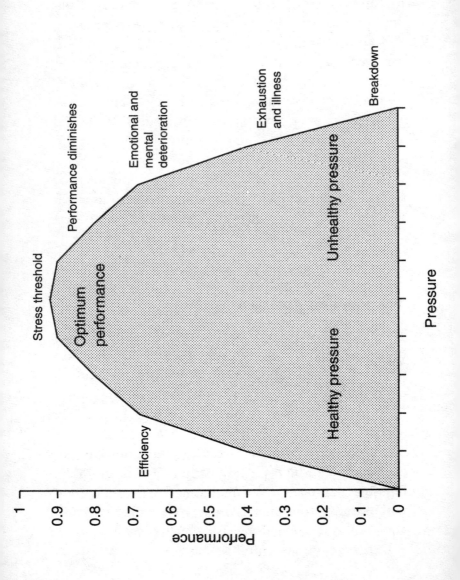

threshold' – when instead of helping your performance, increased pressure begins to make it deteriorate. The emotional, mental and physical stresses begin to take their toll as you feel that you're losing control and can no longer cope.

Everyone's stress threshold is unique. What is easy to handle for one person can prove to be a real stress-inducer for someone else. And to make things even more complicated, your stress threshold isn't static either. What is easy to cope with one day can cause tremendous stress on another. It all depends on a host of interlocking factors.

Stress check: how well are you coping?

The chart below sets out some of the most common symptoms of differing pressure levels. Individually, one or two negative symptoms aren't a cause for worry, but put together they give a good overall picture of how you're coping.

Wherever you are on the scale, it is important to listen to what your body is telling you, and to respond accordingly.

• If you ticked mostly boxes in the far left-hand column, you are not being stimulated by your job. Improving your time management skills won't necessarily help much. Perhaps it's time to look for another job, or make some radical changes to your working environment.

What is your body telling you about your current pressure level? Tick the appropriate boxes:

Too little pressure	Optimum pressure	Too much pressure	Burnout-level pressure
❏ Tired	❏ Creative	❏ Anxious	❏ Exhausted
❏ Apathetic	❏ Vital	❏ Tense	❏ Unable to concentrate
❏ Bored	❏ Confident	❏ Forgetful	❏ Constantly ill
❏ Lethargic	❏ Effective	❏ Tired	❏ Impotent/frigid
❏ Passive	❏ In control	❏ Worried	❏ Emotionally drained
❏ Coasting	❏ Satisfied	❏ Headachey	❏ Mentally drained
❏ Under-stimulated	❏ Alert	❏ Sexually indifferent	❏ Physically drained
❏ Hungry	❏ Clear-headed	❏ Unattractive	❏ Deeply depressed

- If you ticked mostly boxes in the centre left column, the amount of pressure you're under is about right for bringing your creativity and vitality fully into your work. Stick with it!

- If you ticked mostly boxes in the centre right column, then the lessons spelled out in this book should help you bring your life back under control. If you are disciplined and careful, you will be able to tick mostly boxes in the centre left column very soon.

- If you ticked mostly boxes in the far right-hand column ('Burnout-level pressure'), talk to the person to whom you're accountable *and* your GP – today.

11

Controlling Stress

The symptoms of stress can provide you with valuable early warning signals which, if you learn to listen to them, can protect you from serious long-term physical, mental or emotional problems. Tragically, most people only ever recognise the symptoms of stress when they hit crisis point. The amount of work and pressure people can cope with constantly varies, depending on a whole set of different factors. It's not just deadlines or outside demands that determine how well we can cope, but the cumulative effect of all that has happened to us up to that point.

Sadly, the pressures we are under rarely allow us to rest or relax when we need to. As a result, we end up feeling trapped, with no obvious means of escape. So our stress level begins to increase even more. Part of effective time management is learning to understand the way you tick and to listen to what your body is telling you. This means learning to make some tough short-term decisions, designed to develop your self-control and pace for optimum efficiency, in order to improve your long-term effectiveness.

Creating the right balance between work, rest and play is vital if you're going to be able to handle pressure well.

The decisive factors

Stress is caused by a combination of three factors:

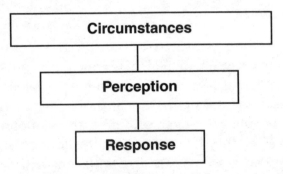

Many people assume that circumstances alone determine our response, but the truth is that circumstances have to go through the filter of our perception, and it is our *perception* of events, rather than the events themselves, that determines our reaction. 'People are disturbed, not by things, but by the view they take of them,' said Epictetus in the first century. In other words, we are never simply 'victims of circumstance'.

If you are late for a very important meeting, for example, being stuck in a traffic jam on the M25 can seem like a disaster; but for a young couple just about to be parted for several months, it can seem like a heaven-sent opportunity to spend a few last precious moments together. And even when we find the situation frustrating, we can reduce our stress levels simply by changing the way we view it, creatively managing our reaction towards it. For instance, if you *are* stuck in a traffic jam on the M25 en route to a crucial meeting, you can use the time to clarify your thoughts about what you are going to say, dictate some letters, or even (if you have a mobile phone with a hands-free set) make a few calls – including one to whomever you're going to meet, of course, telling them you will be late.

Fight or flight

Another ingredient that helps to explain the cumulative effect of stress is what has become known as the 'fight or flight syndrome'. When a situation poses a threat, your body automatically responds by preparing to take action, dealing with it either by staying to fight or by running away as fast as possible. This reaction, common to all animals and triggered by your nervous system, affects virtually all of your body's major organs and functions.

When our ancestors were faced with a bear, wolf or some other physical danger – and it was a case of either stand and fight or beat a hasty retreat – this 'pre-programmed' reaction was an obvious advantage. Our problem is that most of the threats we experience today are psychological rather than physical, yet our natural reaction remains the same. That is why our heart thumps, our muscles tense and our adrenaline pumps savagely round our bodies whenever we have crucial meetings to attend, important phone calls to make or awkward customers or colleagues to deal with. Our bodies are preparing to run for their lives or fight to the death . . . even though such a response would probably be not just unusual but highly inappropriate!

After any episode of immediate stress, it can take anything from a few minutes to several hours for our bodies to calm down and recover, depending on the intensity of our reaction. This begins to prove very difficult if we haven't had time to recover from one adrenaline rush before the next one hits. Our bodies are sent into a semi-permanent state of 'red alert', and as the stress starts to take its toll, our physical and emotional systems will become strained to breaking point, eventually beginning to malfunction.

All this is compounded by the fact that the more stressed you become, the more your defences are broken down and the more vulnerable you are to further stress in the immediate future. Eventually, the kind of pressure you could once have handled with no problem at all will become an intolerable burden. In the end, a relatively minor event may prove enough to be 'the straw that breaks the camel's back'.

Seven steps to regaining control

If you are suffering from the consequences of having passed beyond your stress threshold, or have a tendency to live on the unhealthy side, you should take serious stock of your situation now. By learning to recognise the symptoms of stress early, you can minimise its destructive effects. The symptoms are your body's way of asking you to re-examine your priorities.

The following seven steps are all ways to help you control your stress levels, moving you back towards a healthier, more enjoyable and more effective lifestyle.

1 **Slow down.** When pressure increases, the first thing most of us do is speed up. But if this pattern continues, we can reach a stage of near panic, rushing around from one thing to another but achieving very little. Most successful people seem to share a common ability to control their own pace, unflustered by other people's attempts to speed up the action. If your day is beginning to reach an unproductive speed, do something drastic enough to break the cycle, even if it's only taking a ten-minute break to walk around the block, chat to your colleagues or make a cup of coffee. If your general pace of life is unproductively fast, think of pro-active ways of relaxing and gaining more control rather than reacting to the pressure of circumstances.

2 **Be realistic.** If you are constantly setting yourself unrealistic goals in the vain hope that you can squeeze a few more than twenty-four hours into your day, you are going to be continually frustrated and disappointed. Taking on too much will make you feel hassled and rushed. As a result, your performance will suffer and you are unlikely to make good decisions.

3 **Learn to say 'no'.** Saying 'no' can be one of the hardest things to do, in any environment. You run the risk of seeming unco-operative or unable to cope with your workload. You may even lose some of your popularity. But the benefits of occasionally saying 'no' can be enormous – and not just for you. By taking on jobs you shouldn't, you are inevitably going to produce work of a lower quality than you would otherwise, since you won't have enough time to give due attention to the old ones. So someone somewhere is going to get short-changed. If you say 'no', the job will go to someone else, who may well be able to give it the time it deserves. When you do say 'no', however, don't feel you have to come up with a whole host of excuses: just say 'no', briefly explaining that you do not currently have time to do the project justice.

4 **Take time to reflect.** Taking the time to reflect on your life, and spending time listening to God, helps you put things into perspective. Something that may have felt like a total disaster when it happened can seem much less catastrophic if you widen your

focus to incorporate the bigger picture. 'Quiet times', reflection and planning sessions are often the first to go when the screw really begins to turn. But although they are never a substitute for action, they are an enormous asset when it comes to keeping a true sense of perspective on life. They help us to prioritise things more effectively to make the best use of our limited resources.

5 **Get a balance.** Times of pressure, when the adrenaline is pumping, need to be balanced with quieter times to allow the body to revitalise. Try to create a healthy balance between work, play, friends and family. Variety really *is* the spice of life. Going flat out all the time inevitably produces dullness and eventual burnout.

6 **Enjoy yourself.** What do you do for enjoyment? When did you last take a holiday? The original intention of 'holy-days' was that they should be times of mental, physical and spiritual recreation. Breaks of all sorts have a rejuvenating effect on us: from going to the cinema to reading, from listening to relaxing music to gardening, and from watching sports to playing in them. Everyone's idea of a good time is different, so find something you enjoy. Of course, taking time out can sometimes require a bit of effort if you're really going to feel the benefits. They say that a change is as good as a rest, but it's often better. Try to do one thing you positively enjoy every day, no matter how insignificant it may seem. Rather than being a

'waste' of time, by helping you to bring your stress levels under control it will actually improve your productivity! And by slowing you down a bit, it can also help you gain more enjoyment from what you're already doing.

7 **Take care of yourself.** Sleep, diet and exercise are all important factors in basic stress management. Unless you look after your body, you won't be able to perform at your best. Do you know how much sleep you need? (Most people need an average of eight hours a night, but it varies from person to person.) Do you get it? 'Burning the candle at both ends' may work in the short term, but it will spell disaster in the long run. Exercise is another key area. Many people claim to be too busy to exercise, but regular exercise, despite consuming lots of energy initially, increases your stamina and provides great long-term psychological benefits. Taking regular exercise will help you live a more full and healthy life, improving your efficiency and increasing your ability to cope with stress. A well-balanced diet is also very important. Skipping meals and eating junk food won't help you at all: food feeds the brain as well as the body. Make sure you eat plenty of fresh fruit or vegetables every day. If you look after yourself, both your body and your mind will feel fitter, more alert and more resilient to the damaging effects of pressure.

12

Beating Burnout

If you push yourself beyond your stress threshold, life becomes a vicious circle. All of a sudden, events, your reactions to them and your health begin to have an accelerating negative effect on each other. Once this happens, compensating by working longer hours, taking stimulants (e.g. caffeine), replacing thought with effort, and withdrawing from family and friends, only serve to accelerate the decline.

In most cases, people ignore the effects of stress, even though they're experiencing them. Few of those who could really benefit from stress seminars ever go . . . unless, that is, they've been sent by someone else. Stress is hard to face up to. People under severe stress often avoid having to admit that they have a problem. It is easier to bottle things up in the vain hope that they will disappear. Perhaps afraid that an honest recognition of their condition could itself push them over the edge, they would rather ignore their predicament and hope that it will eventually just go away.

The beginning of the end . . . for stress

The good news is, if you're reading this book because you feel tortured by stress, you have overcome the first hurdle by identifying the problem. Now the next step is to realise that there *is* hope. The following steps are useful guidelines for breaking out of the stress spiral.

1 **Identify the problems.** Identifying the underlying factors that helped cause your stress can be hard, especially since the stress itself can cripple your ability to think clearly. But the source of your stress has to be confronted if anything is going to change, since any solution would otherwise just treat the symptom, not the disease. Write down the three biggest stress factors in your life at the moment. They will almost certainly be a mixture of work-related, home-related and health-related factors.

   i ....

   ii ....

   iii ....

2 **Talk it over.** As BT are fond of saying, 'It's good to talk.' Some people convince themselves that nothing can be done about their situation, and so believe there is little point in talking about it. But

talking about your situation can actually release you from the feeling of being trapped, as well as giving someone else the opportunity to present you with possible options you hadn't considered. Identifying the main causes of your stress can sometimes give you some indication of who is the best person to talk to. It could be your partner, a close friend, a counsellor, your boss, your GP or your pastor. In the case of each of the stress factors you've identified, think through paths of action that could help minimise the pressure you are under with someone else's objective input. Being honest and real, both with other people and with God, is crucial. Whatever you do, don't be tempted to believe that because you're a Christian, you should somehow be able to cope better than anyone else. The Bible is full-to-bursting with people who found handling the pressure difficult: Moses and Elijah, the two greatest prophets of the Old Testament, were both prone to bouts of deep depression. That they found a way through should give us hope, not make us feel guilty for sharing their gloom.

3 **Take action.** This will probably mean taking tough, short-term decisions for the sake of your future effectiveness. Would it help you to get away for a few days? Are there any activities or res-ponsibilities you could drop or pass on to someone else, at least for a while? Having a small group of trusted friends can help ease the pressure,

deflecting things for a short period of time. If you're concerned about your health (e.g. high blood pressure, headaches, heart problems, dizzy spells, weight gain, weight loss or an ulcer), make an appointment to see your GP. As well as allaying your fears, it could help give you the motivation you need to change.

4 **Review your priorities.** Once you start moving beyond 'crisis management', you are in a much better place to take a look at your lifestyle more objectively. What changes do you need to make in order to avoid a repeat of this situation? What does your use of time say about your priorities in life? Reread Section 1 of this book, which takes a closer look at determining your priorities.

5 **Review your time management skills.** Once you are clearer about what are the right things to be doing, you can reduce your stress levels even further by learning how to do them in a more efficient way. Reread Section 2 of this book, which is all about the different practical ways of doing this.

Go For It!

This book is written with one goal in mind: to help you turn your God-given dreams into reality. As the founding director of a Christian charity, I know from personal experience that, for all our belief in God's providential care, Christians are anything but immune from the trials of life or the pressures of our age.

Very often, when our plans and dreams come to nothing, we perform the kind of hasty post-mortem that concludes that we didn't pray enough about them, or that the devil intervened to scupper them, or even that they weren't really 'of God' in the first place. Much of the time, however, they fail for an altogether simpler reason, and one that a more thorough and less 'spiritually' conditioned post-mortem would have shown up all too clearly: we manage our time and resources very badly.

Learning to make the most of your time is a slow process, and there is always room for improvement. The principles and practical advice given in this book can help you to make maximum use of the time you have available to you. But don't make the mistake of following them slavishly. Some of them will help you, others won't. Some will work at various times of your life, and not others.

Every golfer who has ever set foot on a fairway has had just one dream: a hole-in-one. In fact, more often than not, their dream is for eighteen holes-in-one! The fact that they have never achieved it doesn't put them off or send them into bouts of depression. Instead, in a healthy way, their dream spurs them on to improve their game next time around.

Time management is a bit like golf. Don't let the fact that you're never doing it all perfectly put you off or daunt you. Instead, let it spur you on. If you end up putting just 20 per cent of the principles contained in this book into action long term, that's a big step forward. If you were to aim for eighteen holes-in-one and achieve only one, you'd still walk back to the club house very happy. It should be the same with time management.

Aim high, but always remember that time management skills are your servant, not your master. They should empower you to work better and achieve the right balance in your life, not imprison you with guilt.

Making a Team Work

by Steve Chalke

Are you responsible for leading a team? Do others look to you for direction? Do you want others to reach their full potential?

The effectiveness of any team depends upon the quality of its leader. Steve Chalke offers practical advice for anyone who wants to be a better team leader, whether in the local church, in business or in the wider community. He gives guidelines on:

- understanding the importance of teamwork
- the art of delegation
- being accountable
- positive decision-making
- resolving conflict

Kingsway Publications

The Truth About Suffering

by Steve Chalke

This book looks at the eternal question, 'How can God be all-loving and all-powerful and yet there still be suffering in the world?'

We try to resolve the dilemma in different ways, but in the last analysis, God has done something about suffering by becoming human and taking the blame himself. If in Jesus he has done this, then we must follow his example.

Steve Chalke details eight areas in which individuals and Christians can become involved in order to alleviate suffering. Three different levels of commitment are featured, and the areas covered include, among others, debt, disability, unemployment and homelessness.

 **Kingsway Publications**

Battle for the Mind

by David Holden

'Do not conform any longer to the pattern of this world, but be transformed by the renewing of your mind.' Romans 12:2.

Are you defeated by temptation? Dominated by fears from the past? Do you find you can't shake off self-pity or a sense of rejection?

We are surrounded by pressures which, if succumbed to, influence our minds and our thinking in ungodly ways. David Holden says that we are what we think and that is why it is so vital for our minds to be renewed.

This book aims to help you begin to reach out for all the potential that is yours in Christ and make it your own. His desire is to see a generation transformed by the renewing of their minds, changing the world to the glory of God.

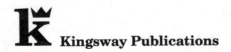 **Kingsway Publications**

Stress: The Challenge to Christian Caring

by Gaius Davies

'We are not, as Christian believers, exempt from any of the stresses that affect anyone else. Our faith is not a passport to freedom from pressures.'

Stress is built into modern life. With sweeping changes in society and technology, our lives move ever more frantically. Using numerous examples from his many years' experience in clinical practice, Dr Davies examines the causes of breakdown and the many sources of stress which exist today: bereavement, guilt, personality problems, sexual tensions and the perennial problem of anxiety.

A book to encourage those suffering from breakdown or stress, prevent others from succumbing to it, and provide invaluable help to counsellors.

 **Kingsway Publications**